Heart & Soul
of the Train

*Personal travel notes
from an
Amtrak attendant*

by Mauris L. Emeka

Mauris L. Emeka

2/17/2000

**Apollo Publishing International
Port Orchard, Washington**

Copyright © 1999 by Mauris L. Emeka

Apollo Publishing International
Box 1937
Port Orchard, Washington (98366)

Cover photo by Pam Sternerson.
Cover design by Edwina Cusolito.

Publisher's Cataloging in Publication

Emeka, Mauris L.
    Heart and soul of the train / by Mauris L.
    Emeka -- 1st ed.
    p. cm.
ISBN: 0-9640125-5-3

        1. Emeka, Mauris L.   2. Train attendants --
    United States -- Biography.   3. Pullman porters --
    United States -- Biography.   4. Afro-American train
    attendants -- Biography.   5. Railroad travel -- United
    States.   I. Title.

    TF140.E44 1999   385.22'092
                            QB199-384

Dedication

Heart & Soul of the Train is dedicated to those AMTRAK on-board service workers who truly "make it happen," three hundred sixty-five days a year.

This book is primarily about unique experiences recorded by the author while working as a train attendant traveling AMTRAK's western routes. It ends with answers to commonly-asked questions regarding train travel in the USA.

Acknowledgements

I wish to express my sincere thanks and deep appreciation to my wife, Sunday Emeka, who helped to inspire the early stages of this book; to Rachael Bennett, Debra Munn, and Vivian Phillips Scott who assisted in editing it; to Ron Snowden of Graphics West in Seattle, Washington for typesetting and layout; and to Edwina Cusolito for the cover design. Apollo Publishing International, however, assumes full responsibility for any errors of omission or commission.

Mauris Emeka . . . often referred to as "Harmonica Man". Drawing by Justin Emeka.

About The Author

Mauris L. Emeka has enjoyed trains since he was a boy growing up in Arkansas and Texas. This is his second book about train travel. A former AMTRAK train attendant and retired Army officer, he is married and the father of four sons. Mauris lives with his family on the Olympic Peninsula near Port Orchard, Washington.

Preface

Having been on the train as a passenger at the age of six to go visit my grandparents, I enjoy Mauris Emeka's stories because they bring back memories I had long forgotten.

Mauris, however, goes far beyond fond memories and enters into the hearts of those he has met along the way. He also shares with readers a warm, compassionate, and spiritual side of himself that truly shines through the entire book.

It has been my pleasure and privilege to help on this heart-opening adventure.

Rachael Bennett
Great Falls, Montana
January 1999

The Pioneer, awaiting departure from the Denver, Colorado Union Station.

Introduction

I hired on as a train attendant with AMTRAK in the Fall of 1989. From the outset, I realized that this would be an unusual endeavor, one in which I would experience a number of memorable moments – exciting adventures, good times, and some not so good. It soon became apparent that I would have to make continual adjustments: First, adjusting to life on the railroad while on a six day trip, then returning home and getting used to a totally different routine for a few days, only to make the switch again back to life on the railroad. These changes offered some unique challenges and opportunities.

Since my early years as an Air Force communications officer, I've been inclined to write. So when I began working on the railroad, it seemed only natural to record my experiences as time and energy would allow.

It's therapeutic whenever I am able to go within and discover ways to associate written words with things occurring around me. I frequently relate better to extraordinary experiences when I write about them. Sometimes, events on the train would happen so fast and in such a way that I had little opportunity to record them at the time. But near the end of the day, just before falling asleep, I would often reflect on that day by recording various thoughts that came to mind. The exercise of writing it on paper was beneficial, because it relieved the stress that often accompanied a nineteen to twenty hour-a-day work schedule.

In contrast to my earlier book, AMTRAKing, this book (except for the final chapter) focuses less on how to travel by train and more on my experiences and personal thoughts as a veteran trainman.

I worked on board until March 1998, at which time I resigned, hoping to spend more time with my family and to pursue writing and free enterprise endeavors. What follows is mainly a collection of personal notes recorded during my years on the railroad.

I hope that readers will find this book stimulating and useful.

. . . and who knows, perhaps we'll see you on the rails someday!

Mauris Emeka
Port Orchard, Washington
Summer 1999

Contents

About the Author iv

Preface v

Introduction vii

The Soul of the Train 1

I. **Working On The Railroad**
    Bussing Around a Derailment 4
    Bathroom Detail 7
    A Ticklish Situation 9
    Safety first 11
    Gotta Have My Harmonica 15
    On Layover in Chicago 18
    . . . It's Not All Roses 22

II. **Other Memorable Experiences with**
    Passengers
    Passenger Carry-By Incident 26
    Passengers as Spiritual Teachers...   29
    A Fellow Writer...from Dallas 30
    Stevie Who?? I Don't Care if You're Little
        Richard! 32
    Perspectives from Fellow Travelers 34
    America's Fast Food 39
    Dirty Laundry 40
    From the Train to the Plane 41
    Coach and Sleeping Car Attendants 44
    My First Trip in the New Employee
        Dormitory Car 46

Tapestry of Train Topics 48
An Old Soldier Relates a World II
    Experience 50
Conversing with Seniors 53
Determination to Restore Health 55
An Emotional Departure from
    Los Angeles 57
Pickup in the Rain 59

III. The Rails...and the Spirit Revealed
The Question of Money 64
Regarding our Children 66
Thoughts Along The Way 67
Race . . . a Slippery Concept 68
Other Random thoughts 70
On the Railroad . . . in the Flow of Grace,
    April 1993 71
Just Before Falling Asleep . . .
    February 25, 1995 72
Feeling Stress 73
Memorable Words of a Fellow Traveler 75
Mother Dear's Passing 76

IV. The "How To" of Traveling by Train
Questions & Answers 80
A Few AMTRAK Facts 95

**What I'll Always Remember and Like About
the Train** 97

A Closing Note 99

Order Form 101

The Soul of the Train

Sometime in January 1991, I recorded the following in my travel notes:

I have always loved the look of the train, the graceful way it rounds the turns through Colorado's Gore Canyon, or as it makes its way through beautiful Glacier National Park in Montana. This "iron horse" on wheels has a magic not easily captured in words or pictures. I thoroughly enjoy interacting with the people on board. Whether we call them passengers or train crew members, to me they are all simply fellow travelers.

The train is more than just another form of public conveyance – it is people of all varieties relating to one another. In our society we're often alienated from our neighbors because of arbitrary things such as age, gender, profession, skin color, social status, and the like. But on-board the train, there's less evidence of the artificial walls that divide us. Instead, we're all just people going somewhere, and most of us are having fun.

Whenever I am rested and not feeling the stress of five or six days on the road, I sincerely enjoy observing families and friends relating to each other, and I enjoy the ever changing scenery outside. The smell of delicious food from the diner is also a special treat, as is the comradeship that is generally felt amongst crew and passengers alike.

All in all, what is most satisfying is seeing people who were previously strangers and who are usually separated into various markets based on age, social class, geography, and gender, now freely intermingling with one another on-board the train. This is rare in a consumer-oriented society such as ours, where people are often divided according to separate markets to further the short term goals of business.

CHAPTER ONE

Working On The Railroad

Bussing Around a Derailment

All of AMTRAK's western trains share the tracks with freight trains. And although freight train derailments are rare, they occasionally happen, and cause AMTRAK trains to experience delays. One such freight derailment occurred on a sunny Spring afternoon in 1994 when I was working on the Empire Builder. We were traveling westbound through North Dakota in what had been a fairly routine trip. The scenery was beautiful rolling plains, with lush vegetation covering the fields as far as the eye could see.

Train Station in Whitefish, Montana

Inside our train, passengers were relaxed, as most of them sat enjoying the big sky overhead, and the rugged mountain peaks in the far distance. But the mood was suddenly broken when the conductor announced on the PA that a freight train accident had occurred ahead of us and that we would have to be bussed around the accident site to another AMTRAK train waiting to continue us on our trip. Following are notes I recorded that day, mainly because I wanted to share the experience with my wife, Sunday, and our ten year old son, Apollo:

It was late afternoon on April 2nd, and we were westbound through North Dakota. Upon our arrival in Williston, North Dakota, the conductor announced that a freight train had derailed ahead of us and that all persons on board would have to be bussed around the derailment.

Transferring from a spacious and comfortable Superliner onto the crowded confines of a bus was quite a contrast, and having to ride about five hours in such cramped quarters can try a person's patience. But my fellow travelers stayed in reasonably good spirits, as crew members explained the situation and reassured everyone that things were okay, and that we would soon board another train to continue our trip. Six buses in all carried us nearly two hundred miles around the derailment site to the town of Havre, Montana. Everyone was given a complimentary box lunch, and in the bus where I rode, we sang 50s and 60s hit tunes, all accompanied by my harmonica.

Some travelers were undoubtedly disappointed by this unscheduled disruption, but when you work on the rails, you come to accept such an experience as "all in a day's work." On this day, the attitude of the train crew set the tone, and passengers made the best of the experience. We arrived into Havre just after midnight, and all were eager to return to the train which waited at the station to continue us on our westward trip.

Retiring to my room in the dormitory car that night, I was reminded of how on-board crewmembers consistently work together to get a job done. I laid down, and in virtually no time the rhythmic motion of the train carried me to slumber land.

Bathroom Detail

Each Superliner Coach car has five or six bathrooms. Train attendants, therefore, get a good workout keeping them clean and functioning during the course of a long distance trip. I was a bit apprehensive about cleaning bathrooms when I first went to work for AMTRAK in 1989. After all, public bathrooms are sometimes not the most inviting. This hesitation, however, was short-lived.

On my second or third trip working the sleeper car, a shower connection in an upstairs deluxe bedroom sprung a leak. Before I figured out how to stop the water, the bathroom in the upstairs bedroom, as well as two downstairs bathrooms, had flooded. When something like this happens en route, there's no plumber to come to the rescue; so you simply do the best you can with what you have. I finally stopped the leak by locating the main valve and shutting it off; then I proceeded to dry out the upstairs bathroom/ shower compartment. Later, I cleaned and dried out the two downstairs bathrooms, using hand towels to soak up the water and wipe the rooms down from ceiling to floor.

After that nearly two-hour ordeal, I was thoroughly initiated into the task of bathroom cleaning, and was now confident that bathroom cleaning duties would no longer pose a problem for me.

A Ticklish Situation

There was once a man in my coach who had an especially delicate problem – his feet smelled when he pulled his shoes off! After receiving complaints from nearby passengers, I tried tactfully to ask the man to put his shoes back on. He did as he was asked, but even with his shoes on, his feet continued to smell like sour onions in a dirty clothes box. Passengers continued to complain to me, and one of them finally called in the conductor, who told the man with the offensive feet that he might have to be put off the train.

Now, even though this man had become the center of attention because of an embarrassing hygiene problem, he remained jovial and upbeat – even apologetic and humble. So instead of removing the man from the train, the conductor asked me to offer to let him go to the dormitory car to take a shower. I did just that, and the man accepted my offer. Upon returning to his seat from the shower, however, the odor was still there, though it was less offensive. I then requested that he sit in the lounge car. He finished his trip chatting and making laughter with others in the lounge car.

As one of my elementary school teachers used to say, a smile and a lighthearted attitude go a long way! Had the man with smelly feet been more difficult to deal with, the conductor surely would have thrown him off the train. But this passenger's attitude and demeanor made all the difference. Reflecting on the situation later that day, I was reminded that much of life depends on the attitude with which one approaches it.

Safety First

Following is a brief account I wrote on the morning of September 15, 1994, traveling northbound on the Coast Starlight:

I awoke this morning at about 5:30 to discover that we have been sitting in the same spot for nearly two hours. The reason is that our train collided with a car left abandoned on the tracks. We were about forty miles south of Redding, California, and at impact we were traveling only about thirty-five miles per hour. Only when our train rounded a curve did the engineer see the car, but he did not have enough distance to stop the train. The car was completely demolished in the crash, but luckily, no one was injured. Before we could proceed, however, debris had to be removed from the tracks, our locomotive was inspected, and reports had to be filed. I couldn't help thinking how insensitive and uncaring someone would have to be to leave an automobile on

Never Drive Around The Gates
If the gates are down, stop and stay in place. Do not cross the tracks until the gates are raised and the lights have stopped flashing.

the tracks where the train engineer could not possibly see it in time to stop.

Obviously, safety is a big issue on the railroad. A train takes a considerably longer distance to stop than a car, and the impact of any resulting crash is so much greater due to the train's weight. Considering the number of miles AMTRAK trains travel every day, they have a very good safety record, and of the accidents that do occur, a large percentage are railroad crossing accidents caused by a vehicle driver who attempts unsuccessfully to beat the train.

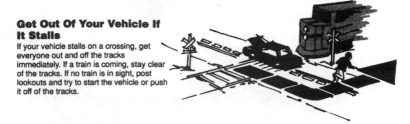

Get Out Of Your Vehicle If It Stalls
If your vehicle stalls on a crossing, get everyone out and off the tracks immediately. If a train is coming, stay clear of the tracks. If no train is in sight, post lookouts and try to start the vehicle or push it off of the tracks.

During my years working on the railroad, I was in four accidents – one caused by the abandoned car on the tracks, two caused by vehicle drivers who ignored the crossing gates, and one occurred when a young girl deliberately walked in front of the train .It's rare that many people on board are injured. Deep inside I always found these experiences

very unsettling, in spite of the fact that out-
wardly I was obliged as a crew member to do
my best to project a cool and calm demeanor.

A word of advice: Don't try to beat the train
at a railroad crossing, as that can be danger-
ous business. And if you find yourself inside
a vehicle that stopped on the railroad tracks,
simply get out of the vehicle at once!

LOOK,
LISTEN...

AND
LIVE!

The harmonica, my constant companion while on the road.

Gotta Have My Harmonica

If I remembered nothing else when I got ready to go out on the road, I remembered to bring along my harmonicas. On some trips, I was so busy that I barely got a chance to play them, except when I was standing outside on the station platform. But even when I had no time to play, it was a good feeling just knowing that these handy little companions were there for me. I especially liked harmonicas in the keys of G, A and B flat, because they produce the low-sounding notes that go well with the sound of the train.

I learned to play the harmonica during my second year on-board the train. I had longed to know how to play ever since my high school days as a tuba player in the band. I liked the melodic sounds of the harmonica so well that once I picked up the instrument, I didn't stop until I could make music with it. It was always a special treat to meet another harmonica player on-board, and if they hadn't brought a harmonica along, I would loan them one of mine and urge them to blow a few riffs. That way I could check out some of their techniques and maybe borrow a few musical ideas.

Whenever I didn't get much opportunity to play on the train, I made up for it in my hotel room on layover. This soothing, relaxing, and handy little companion (whether it's a 10-hole blues harp or a 12-hole chromatic) helps me to feel spontaneous and youthful when I'm on the road.

Sometimes it seems like the harmonica goes with the train like a hand and glove. I wrote the following words the morning of December 17, 1993:

"Twas fun playing the harmonica for a few minutes this morning as we pulled off from Whitefish, Montana. As the train gained momentum, it produced a cadence that went well with my harmonica rendition of "When The Saints Go Marchin' In."

Soon the train got up to speed, and the beat of the wheels was too fast to go with the song, but it was sure fun for a few moments.

Along with the rhythmic sound of the wheels, I felt my body moving with the motion of the train, as the harmonica played this beautiful refrain.

Some of the fondest memories of my early years on the railroad are of learning to play the harmonica. The downstairs vestibule area of the Superliner is a perfect place to play tunes to relieve some of the inevitable tensions that build up during the course of a six-day round trip. The harmonica helped to smooth out the emotional highs and lows of life on the road.

On Layover in Chicago

One of the pleasures of working on the railroad was layover time in America's great cities. During eight and a half years, I spent layovers in Chicago, Salt Lake City, Los Angeles, Oakland, Denver, and Eugene and Portland, Oregon. The most memorable layovers were in Chicago, a city rich with things to see and do. In the early years, we had about a twenty-hour layover in Chicago (longer than in any other city), so I was able to visit the famous art museum, take walks along the beautiful lake front beach, and go to an occasional blues night club. I usually partook of these pleasures alone, because that gave me the freedom to be spontaneous and pursue what suited me at any given moment.

Instead of the hotel transport van, I usually took the street bus from Chicago Union Station to the hotel, because that gave me the opportunity to mingle with local people and hear them relate their experiences. Sometimes I would stay at Union Station in Chicago and have a workout at the employee physical fitness center on the second floor. Other times I went directly to the hotel, and from there to a nearby library to study about the Common Law and the Constitution. (A lady whom I befriended on the train in 1994 aroused my interest in early American law and in our Constitution of 1789). At any rate, a twenty-hour layover can go fast in a city that offers so many interesting things to do. After AMTRAK's restructuring in the mid 1990s, our Chicago layover was reduced to about eighteen hours, and later to about 16 hours – much to my regret.

Also after the restructuring, train attendants for Superliner coach cars were required to work not one but two (and sometimes three) coaches. Here are some typical duties of a train attendant in an AMTRAK Superliner coach: assisting travelers on and off the train, insuring that people de-train at their proper destinations, passing out pillows, keeping five or six bathrooms in each car clean and functioning, cleaning up after motion sickness children, fetching dinners for handicapped travelers, monitoring the car for general cleanliness and temperature control, and assisting passengers in any way possible in case of an emergency. Sometimes, just keeping the bathrooms clean and in working order can be challenging enough, so when we were assigned two coach cars, this exactly doubled our workload, with no increase in hours to accomplish such a thing. Having two cars to work also increased the possibility of a "carry-by," (that is, someone not getting off the train at the proper stop), and train attendants are usually faulted here, even though the conductor is officially responsible. From my vantage point as a train attendant, the reduced layover time, and the additional coaches to look after all made the six-day Chicago round trip more stressful, and considerably less fun.

But I always looked forward to a layover. Once while waiting for a street bus in Chicago, I struck up a conversation with a man who was from Fargo, Arkansas, which is where I was born and spent most of my formative years. He knew my mother's family there in Fargo, and spoke highly of my grand-father Mahon, who was one of the founders of this small all African American community in northeast Arkansas.

On another occasion, while on layover in Denver, I met an interesting older woman at the library who bore a close resemblance to the underground railroad organizer, Sojourner Truth. She said she had no home, and that she had raised twelve children, eight of her own and four foster children. When I asked her why wouldn't she go live with one of her children, she replied that she occasionally does, but that most of the time she prefers to be on her own.

Layover time was always an important part of my railroad experience. Hitting the streets and getting to talk with local people made my layovers more fun.

. . . It's Not All Roses

In the Spring of 1992, a man from a small Idaho town was brought onto my car in a wheelchair. Much to my amazement, this man, who was diabetic and had no legs, was unaccompanied. His destination was Portland, Oregon, about a twelve-hour ride from where he got on the train. I later learned that this overweight man in his thirties was recently released from the hospital for a diabetic condition. I helped him to and from the men's room, brought him food, kept his medicine refrigerated, and looked after his general comfort. My heart went out to him, and I cared for him as best I could, but his needs were beyond what I or other train crew members could give. Someone had apparently put this gentleman on the train, thinking that the train crew could look after all of his needs. Eventually, the conductor on board had no choice but to call ahead for an ambulance to carry him off the train in eastern Oregon, where he could receive adequate care.

When you work on the train, you do what you have to in dealing with various situations. Whenever faced with a challenging situation like the one just described, I would often think, "what if this were my brother, father, mother or some other loved one?". Whenever I would think in those terms, it automatically motivated me to give good service (from the heart).

Portland, Oregon's 100-year-old Union Station.

CHAPTER TWO

Other Memorable Experiences With Passengers

Passenger Carry-By Incident

We arrived at Lincoln, Nebraska, on the California Zephyr at about 7 o'clock one September morning of 1990. Twice I walked the length of both coach cars, announcing, "This is Lincoln," "This is Lincoln." But the lady in seat number 16 bound for Lincoln was asleep, and I failed to get her off at this stop. The last time I walked by her seat when I canvassed the car, I tapped her and said, "Ma'am, we're in Lincoln." She moved slightly, so I thought she would get up and de-train. I then went downstairs to help other passengers, thinking that the lady in seat 16 would also be coming down. But she never came downstairs to exit the train, and I did not realize she was still on board until we left Lincoln.

Needless to say, it's always stressful for all concerned when something like this happens. As a train attendant, you do your best to insure that each traveler gets off at the proper destination. But occasionally a "carry-by" will occur, particularly in light of the demands placed on train crew members. When this happens, AMTRAK generally takes responsibility for returning that passenger back to his or her proper station stop.

My primary concern and regret was that a passenger was inconvenienced, and was (understandably) stressed out about it. Of less concern to me was the fact that the on-board train Chief would record this incident in his report.

Historic King Street Station, Seattle, Washington.
Photo by Gabriel Emeka.

Passengers as Spiritual Teachers . . . Christmas Eve, 1995

Following is the gist of a conversation I had with a fellow traveler while I was working a local train from Seattle to Eugene, Oregon:

I was talking with a woman this day, December 24, 1995, and I told her that sometimes I felt less than exuberant, even out of sorts, at this time of year, since I had to work instead of spending the holiday with my family. She remarked that she averted such feelings herself by finding ways to be of help to others. Her words were, "A person can choose to take their mind off themselves and find a way to help someone else." When she did that, she said, it made a difference in how she felt.

I later realized what valuable opportunities my job often gives me to meet people who, like this woman, are willing to share basic truths for living.

A Fellow Writer...
from Dallas

On this day, September 18, 1997, while working on the Empire Builder, I met a lady whom I will probably never forget. I never did ask her name, I just knew her as a lady in her late 60s or early 70s who was from Dallas, Texas. She was a careful listener, and when she spoke she always seemed to offer a positive comment, no matter what she was speaking about. We talked about family, school, politics, the loss of loved ones, and more. She

would sometimes repeat what I said in her own words, and then ask, "Is that what you meant?" Then she would always reply with what seemed a thoughtful comment. The humility and grace that she exuded made it a joy to converse with her.

As we arrived at Devil's Lake, Minnesota, where she left the train, she was in the process of telling me about a novel she had been working on that essentially deals with turning tragedy into triumph. As this graceful woman with her characteristic Texas accent departed the train, I thanked her heartily for sharing so much.

Just then it occurred to me once again that the train offers an opportunity to meet interesting people who often talk freely about their various life experiences.

Stevie Who?? I Don't Care if You're Little Richard!

On April 1, 1996, I was working the sleeper car on *The Pioneer*, and in one of the economy rooms was a lady named Nancy who grew up in Haslett, Michigan. Sleeping car attendants are required to introduce themselves to their guests shortly after the guests arrive on the train. When I introduced myself to Nancy, we started a conversation, and she said something like, "I bet you get to hear some pretty interesting stories working on the train, don't you?" I replied, "Yes, I get to hear some good ones from time to time." So she said, "Well, here's one for you, and it's a true story:

"In 1963 I was in college. My boyfriend and I had broken up, and I was feeling very low as a result of it. So I decided that in order to get out of the doldrums I would take a bus

home to Kalamazoo, Michigan, for the week-end and get some words of uplift from my parents. While I was sitting on the Greyhound bus feeling depressed and anxious to arrive home , there was a youngster in the seat behind me who kept humming tunes, and every so often I could hear the faint sound of a harmonica riff. I found the harmonica playing and the humming very annoying. I was in no mood to hear any noise, music or not. I was about eighteen years old, and this young lad was about ten or twelve.

"After I had tolerated enough of this kid's music, I turned around and in a very stern voice said: "DO YOU MIND?" He said, "But I'm just practicing, ma'am. I'm Little Stevie Wonder." And not knowing the name "Little Stevie Wonder," I replied, "I don't care if you're Little Richard, just knock it off!" and he did. A bit later, we arrived at Kalamazoo where we both got off the bus. I think this young man was on his way to the state school for the blind located in Kalamazoo. At any rate, when I arrived home and told my brother about the incident, he explained to me that this was in fact the boy wonder of rhythm and blues – the now legendary musician and songwriter, Stevie Wonder.

Perspectives from Fellow Travelers

During one trip I rode with a group from Australia, whose sense of humor and interesting tales kept me laughing. I got the impression that they really liked the USA and identified with it, perhaps because Australia is also a cultural offspring from Great Britain.

On another trip, I got to know a couple from New Zealand. They spoke of how life in their country was simpler and slower-paced than in the USA. The woman traced her ancestry to England, and the husband's ancestors were native to New Zealand, the so-called aboriginal people.

I sometimes received letters from passengers, especially those who read my book, AMTRAKing. A lady from Wisconsin sent me a note on November 18, 1997:

Dear Mr. Emeka,
It was such a pleasure talking with you. Thank you for writing such an informative book. I wish I had read it before traveling on the Lakeshore Limited to Croton-Harmon

from Chicago this past January. Since I am retired and love AMTRAK travel, I'm sure I will refer to it frequently. When I booked my upcoming trip through AMTRAK Vacations (agency) they had me arrive in Chicago three minutes before I was to leave Chicago. Since I wasn't too comfortable with that timing, I'm going to leave Milwaukee on an earlier train. After reading your book and noting suggested time allowances between trains, I'm much more comfortable with my questioning of the arrangements.

P.S. I hope sometime to be on one of your "Trains".

Sincerely,
Mary
Milwaukee, Wisconsin

A man whom I previously rode with wrote to me in December 1997 from Australia:

Dear Mr. Emeka,
What a delight to have ridden by train throughout the western part of the USA. Yours is an incredibly vast country with lots of variety. It was my first time in North America, and I look forward to returning. Although not always on time, your trains are comfortable, and most people seemed hospitable. I particularly enjoyed our conversation about the benefits of "home schooling".
Good luck to you,
David S.
Perth, Australia

The following was received in October 1996:

Dear Mr. Emeka,
While I was waiting in Seattle's King Street Station for the Empire Builder, I decided to run over and check out the Elliott Bay Book Company, specifically to get my own copy of your book, AMTRAKing. I read it in one sitting that first night on the train. It is a great book and a wonderful way to remember the train. My husband and I rode the Pioneer to Seattle, and today is our last day on the Em-

pire Builder back to Chicago. We have had the best time and enjoyed every minute on these trains. I appreciate the time and effort you have taken to write your book as a guide for train passengers. You write well and simply. May God bless you in the future. Possibly we'll meet up on some trip in the next few years.

Yours Truly,
Diana
Brentwood, Tennessee

On July 15, 1997, a fellow traveler came up to me while I was standing on the station platform in Saint Paul/Minneapolis. He started talking to me, and later that morning I recorded our exchange in my trip notes:

I had conversation with a man in his senior years this morning. He said he and his son were en route to Wisconsin to attend a final burial service for his recently deceased wife. "Yes, I'm on a difficult mission," he said, "be-

cause I'm going to LaCrosse to bury my wife this afternoon." He said he and his wife had been married thirty-two years. When he said that, I replied that my wife and I had been married for thirty-one years. He then came closer to me, and with a pleasant but serious expression, he said, "You must always tell your wife you love her. Do it often and without fail." He said, "You know, these girls give us more than we can ever thank them for – the raising of our children, putting up with us, and more." His eyes were a bit teary by this time, though that did not disrupt his soft and purposeful gaze into my eyes. He then said, "When you lose them, it breaks your heart." I nodded in agreement and thanked this kind and sensitive man for his shared comments, assuring him I would take his words to heart.

As I stepped back into the sleeping car to continue preparing rooms for oncoming passengers, I found myself uttering a prayer for this fellow human being grieving the loss of a loved one. I prayed that he would KNOW that God is present, especially in that time of great pain.

America's Fast Food

One morning I talked with a lady from Wales while we were standing on the platform at the Saint Paul/Minneapolis station. She had been riding in my coach car since Seattle. I asked her for her thoughts about the USA, wanting to know how she and people from her country saw ours. She seemed hesitant to speak at first, and then said she was amazed at the amount of junk food and processed food we eat, adding that she had noticed many overweight people. She also expressed amazement at the cheap prices on food, and at the fact that there are so many places to buy it. Americans are very much into America, she said, and there's not much news about other countries. Lastly, she said, the USA seems violence prone – it seemed to her that we try to control people and things with violence, or threats of it, and that we seem to be amused by both acts of violence or discussions of it, in ways she could not understand.

Dirty Laundry

Not every view from the train reveals America's scenic beauty. It's early morning this July 15, 1994, and we're approaching metropolitan Sacramento, California, on the Coast Starlight. On both sides of the train one can see trash, abandoned cars, and other less than picturesque scenes. For all the beautiful and enticing scenery that we promote as part of train travel, there are also sights that are less attractive.

Our train is now well within Sacramento's city limits, and under the railroad overpasses one can see a few homeless shelters. Ever wonder where worn-out commercial waste, such as old signs and wooden pallets, end up? When you take a ride on the train, you can enjoy great views, certainly, but you also get to see rear ends of buildings and stores that may look pretty out front, yet whose dirty laundry is out back.

From the Train to The Plane

I once worked as a dining car waiter from Seattle to Minneapolis in May 1994. At the end of this stint, AMTRAK flew me back to Seattle in time to be ready for the next day's regular work as a train attendant. I therefore went from the train directly to the plane, and what a difference there is between the two! All things considered, I definitely prefer the train.

The most noticeable difference between the train and the plane is the experience of actually riding on them. Though the plane on which I rode was a wide-bodied Boeing 747, the seats were packed so tightly that there was very little leg or elbow room. There were over three hundred passengers on this three-hour nonstop flight. Unlike on the train, people did not seem especially lively or talkative, and I saw apprehension on the faces of passengers as I stepped on board the airplane and walked down the aisle to my assigned seat. The atmosphere was also different – some passengers seemed tense, and the air was stuffy. During the flight, a few people talked with each other, but the atmosphere of spaciousness and relaxation that I'm accustomed to on the train was missing. I spoke with the person seated on my left, but our conversation was brief. Flight crew members were friendly, but had little time to spare, as they had meals and other amenities to serve, all in three hours.

I liked the fact that the plane touched down in Seattle so quickly, but in effect I felt that the trip had killed three hours – and I'd prefer not to "kill time." Not interacting with people and being unable to observe the passing scenery gave me an unsettled feeling. But that was part of the price I paid for being able to return to Seattle so soon.

The experience of this plane ride, though it got me from point A to point B in a hurry, reminded me that we're living in a world that seems to be spinning out of control. Our technology enables us to get from place to place quickly and to build buildings and virtually move mountains overnight. But in the meantime, our quality of life suffers.

The train offers an opportunity to slow things down, and to reflect on our consumer-oriented way of life. It enables one to gaze upon the passing countryside in a more natural and relaxed way. If I must get somewhere right away, I'll choose the plane. But if I want to experience life in a more pleasant, unhurried way, the train is my clear choice.

Train Station in Greeley, Colorado

Coach and Sleeping Car Attendants

On the whole, AMTRAK's coach and sleeping car attendants, especially those veterans who have been on the job for many years, rate high marks for service rendered. These men and women are accustomed to meeting the public, they're sensitive to passenger needs, and most are good conversationists. Most attendants are self-starters who have a good sense of ownership in terms of their particular assignment. Whether it is having coffee ready at six in the morning in the sleeper car, keeping the car clean, bringing food and drink to mobility-impaired persons, or responding to an emergency – these men and women are pros at what they do.

In terms of service rendered, I'll select a train attendant over an airline attendant any day of the week. The train attendant usually can take more time to talk with passengers, answer their questions, and exchange stories. They are also resourceful. Suppose, for example, you accidentally tore a button off your coat or blouse. A train attendant could probably find a needle and thread for you. On a long trip, you're more likely to get to know your train attendant, if you desire to do so.

The train attendant is part of a long tradition of service, going back to the days of the Pullman Porters. Passenger train travel in the United States pre-dates commercial flight by about seventy-five years. One reason I accepted the opportunity to work on board was that my Uncle Freeman from Kansas City had been a Pullman Porter during World War II.

Once while traveling between Denver and Chicago, I met a retired Pullman Porter, and it was delightful talking with him. Just before he de-trained, he told me, "No matter what situation you're in, if you can just keep it light, and keep smiling, it'll help you get through it."

It was a pleasure, and indeed a humbling experience, to have talked with this gentle but expressive man of African ancestry, who helped to maintain a tradition of excellent service on the railroad.

My First Trip in the New Superliner II Employee Dormitory Car, February 23, 1994

Many train attendants who work west of Chicago have an unenthusiastic acceptance of the old Santa Fe employee dormitory car. This is the car designated for train crew to rest and lounge in, but its rooms are tiny, its hallway is dark and narrow, and its air is often stuffy. That's why I was pleasantly surprised to arrive at the train today in Seattle to learn that we had a new dormitory car – the Superliner II Transition Sleeper. This new "home on the road" car for crew members is a much welcomed addition to the fleet.

When I walked into this new dorm car for the first time, it was a delight, as I could smell

Superliner employee dormitory car.

the newness of the carpet and observe the bright colors of the decor. I went from room to room examining the upper and lower berths and the sliding doors that opened and closed with ease. Then I went downstairs to check out the crew lounge area and showers. The design of this car seems well thought out. Other crew members also expressed great satisfaction with this handsome replacement for the older Santa Fe dorm cars.

We left Seattle King Street Station on schedule, and shortly after a delicious dinner, I went to the new dorm car and selected a room, then made up my bed and adjusted the heat in the room. This way, once I was finally ready to turn in (sometime just after midnight), my room would be prepared for my return.

I slept comfortably this first night, thanks to the smooth riding and relatively quiet "trucks" (the wheel and axle sets) on this car. My sincere thanks to the Bombardier Company that manufactured this dorm car (#39008), one of the first of many to be put into operation in the coming months. This is one trip that the other crew members and I will surely remember with great fondness.

Tapestry of Train Topics

A lady named Chris from Rexburg, Idaho, once showed me the neatest card trick. I shared it with my son, Apollo, when I got home. He's been fascinated with magic tricks ever since.

On yet another trip I learned from a twenty-four-year-old gentleman how he was able to arrange a leveraged buy out of a large and well-established janitorial service company. He purchased this $300,000 firm using only $6,000 of his own money.

In June 1993, a lady explained to me the benefits of home schooling. She spoke about how it can promote family cohesiveness, foster critical thinking in young people, and provide a setting where they are encouraged to be self-defined. My conversation with this mother of four was a major factor in my wife's and my electing to home school our own son, Apollo, from 1994 to 1998.

On a trip from Chicago to Seattle, a retired schoolteacher explained to me the benefits of something called the common law Pure Trust Organization. She explained that this is a little-known tool for structuring one's personal affairs, and that because it is a common law contract it does not depend on statutes to give it lawful effect. She indicated that the Pure Trust Organization has been successfully used for many decades by the very wealthy to preserve and protect their assets; but that it's usefulness is now being discovered by more and more average, ordinary people. In the months and years that followed, I developed an interest in the Pure Trust, and studying it in great detail, I have since become quite knowledgeable in this area.

An Old Soldier Relates a World War II Experience

On this trip (October 4, 1996) a fellow traveler and former World War II combat veteran
told me about a particularly profound experience. First, he showed me where he had
been shot in the head, and where he had
received shrapnel in the leg while fighting
in the Normandy Invasion. Then he said that
after he'd received a serious injury on the
front line, a Red Cross rescue vehicle picked
him up to carry him to get medical treatment.
The Red Cross vehicle driver said to him, "I
hope you don't mind riding in the back with
an injured German soldier." This old soldier
said he had replied, "Hell no, I will not ride
back there with that so and so," as he felt
intense hatred for anything resembling a
German soldier. So this seriously injured
man settled for sitting up front in the Red
Cross rescue vehicle, although he should
have been lying down in back with the en-
emy German soldier.

Right after the Red Cross vehicle pulled off,
it was hit by a mortar attack, and everyone
inside was killed, except for this one man,

my passenger. He described how gruesome and painful it was to have been on the receiving end of that mortar attack, having to listen to the screaming and moaning of all the men in the vehicle as they met with death. My passenger said he, too, would surely have died had he not been thrown out. He remembered looking at the charred and smouldering vehicle, regretting that he had been unable to save anyone inside before fire and smoke overcame them. "At that moment," he said, "I suddenly felt great empathy for the German soldier as well, and I would have given anything to have gotten all the men out of the burning vehicle. But I myself could hardly move." He went on to say, "I suddenly saw that German soldier as just another human being who wanted so desperately to live."

More than fifty years after the Normandy Invasion, this seventy-seven-year-old combat veteran still appears to experience sorrow and grief when talking about this incident. He said he has asked himself many times over the years why all the others died that day, when his life was spared. Just then, I had to go and assist another passenger; but before I left, the old man said, "It's too bad that so many people today do not really know the price that was paid for the freedoms they enjoy."

Conversing with Seniors

When traveling on the train, I found it easy to engage in conversation with older travelers – those in their fifties and beyond. It was very satisfying, because these travelers often shared what it was like to live in the USA in years gone by. One gentleman explained how he and his family cut timber in Oregon and floated it down the river to the mill. On another trip, a grandmother of eight from a rural town in Maine explained how she and her family made it through the harsh New England winters of the 1930s.

Salem, Oregon Amtrak Station

When I spoke with elderly people on the train, I frequently asked them to describe their principal occupations. "I was a wheat farmer," one would say; "I drove a truck," some else would say. Others replied, "I was a school teacher," "I was a county judge," "I had my own shoe repair shop," or "I raised my five children, then went to work as a waitress." In most instances they shared details of their previous occupations, and other aspects of their lives as well. They explained just what it was like to raise five children in the 1930s and 40s, or what it was like driving trucks across country, or teaching junior math, or presiding as the judge over the county court. Sometimes elderly people traveling alone didn't have much to say, but asking them about their earlier occupations nearly always aroused their interest, and as a result, lively conversation followed.

Too often in our fast-paced society, the elderly are ignored as if they have no function except to occupy a space in a nursing home. Talking on the train with people who had reached their senior years, I was reminded that much of what we take for granted was made possible by those who came before us.

Determination to Restore Health

On January 23, 1994, I was working the sleeping car on The Pioneer when a passenger told me about a recent illness she had experienced. The woman was in her late thirties to early forties, and she had contracted a disease called reflex sympathetic dystrophy syndrome (RSDS), diagnosed by her regular doctor as a rare, incurable disease. After spending about $10,000 on various medical exams and treatments, she had discovered Dr. Harold Klassen, a naturopath in Aberdeen, Idaho. When I spoke with the woman, she was returning home to Wisconsin after spending two weeks in Dr. Klassen's clinic. She told me she was about 95 percent healed, and she expected to be completely well in a month. Her name was Sondra, she said; her husband was a truck driver, and they had two sons, aged 20 and 21.

When Sondra spoke about having been healed from RSDS, her eyes lit up and she looked excited. She said she had gone to more than one medical physician, and each had told her to prepare to live with her condition for the rest of her life. But something inside this calm and composed lady had told her to read and learn as much as she could about RSDS. Sondra said she would encourage all those with an illness to inform themselves thoroughly about the nature of it.

Just before Sondra got off the train in Milwaukee, I remember her saying, "We must take greater responsibility for our own health. Doctors cannot do that for us, no matter how well-intentioned they are." In addition, she said, "It's so important that we acknowledge and respect the healing power within our bodies."

I felt lucky and grateful to have engaged in conversation with this kind and gracious lady. She affirmed my belief that although the professionals can assist us, we each must take responsibility for our own health.

An Emotional Departure from Los Angeles

I was working on the Coast Starlight the morning of October 24, 1994, and shortly after we pulled off from the station, I took a few minutes to record the following:

This morning prior to departing Los Angeles Union Station, a young man walked down the platform to board my coach car. With him were two ladies; I learned later that one was his mother and the other was his grand-

Inner courtyard of the Los Angeles Union Station.

mother. After a few parting remarks, the young man stepped aboard the train and turned to wave goodbye. Just then, his mother stepped onto the train and said, "Give me a goodbye kiss, son." Next, the grandmother stepped onto the train, and in a soft and somewhat stern voice, said, "Always remember to say your prayers." He replied, "I sure will, Grandma." The two women then stepped off the train while this young man of college age proceeded upstairs to find a seat.

As a train attendant, I witness lots of family send-offs. For the most part, they do not phase me one way or the other. But this one left a special impression. The words of the grandmother urging her grandson to be sure to pray – these are the same words my own grandmother would have said. Suddenly, I could hear the reassuring voice of my Grandmother Mahon.

Pickup in the Rain

About a month before I quit the railroad in 1998, I had a memorable conversation with a fellow traveler, a middle-aged woman en route to a small town in Tennessee to be with a terminally ill friend. It was a busy trip for me as train attendant, yet I was able to converse with her off and on between Columbus, Wisconsin and Chicago. We shared accounts of our early years in the rural south, the fact that many people lived close to the land, had a sense of community, and helped one another. At one point, she handed me a

typed piece that someone had forwarded to her over the Internet. Here, Mauris, she said: "...you can have this piece, because it reflects wonderfully on what you and I have been talking about this afternoon." She said she didn't know if it described something that had actually happened or not, but that there was a great lesson in it. Here's how it went:

Late one night at around 11:30, an older African-American woman was standing on the side of an Alabama highway trying to endure a lashing rainstorm. Her car had broken down and she desperately needed a ride. Soaking wet, she decided to flag down the next car. A young white man stopped to help her – an occurrence generally unheard of in those conflict-filled 1960s. The man took her to safety, helped her to get assistance, and put her into a taxicab. She seemed to be in a big hurry! She wrote down his address, thanked him, and the taxi drove away. About seven days later, there was a knock on the man's door. To his surprise, a giant console TV was delivered to his home. A special note was attached. It read:

Thank you so much for assisting me on the highway the other night. The rain drenched not only my clothes but my spirit. Then you came along. Because of you, I was able to make it to my dying husband's bedside just before he passed away. God bless you for helping me and unselfishly serving others.

Signed:
Mrs. Nat King Cole

After reading the above piece, the following occurred to me: It was that my working on-board offered an opportunity to serve others unselfishly, and that I was deeply grateful for the experience.

Green River, Wyoming train station.

Heading southbound along Puget Sound. The Tacoma (Washington) Narrows Bridge stands in the background.

CHAPTER THREE

The Rails . . .
And
The Spirit
Revealed

The Question of Money

Riding on the train afforded me the time and opportunity to do some introspective thinking, especially about matters of Spirit.

Here are thoughts that came to mind while I was on layover in Chicago on September 4, 1993, after learning that I would be furloughed from the railroad as part of a seasonal layoff:

In our materialistic society, it's easy to think that money (and what it can buy) is the source of our happiness and well-being. We think if we could just get enough money, somehow our main problems would be solved. So off we go chasing the greenbacks with great determination, only to learn later that money and material goods are not really the answer.

Through prayer, meditation, and conscious living we realize that our sufficiency is in something greater than material things. Unfortunately, the sense that we are separate from God is what makes us pursue material things with such determination, hoping that they will bring happiness and contentment.

Sure, we require money to get along. But it's so important to keep money in spiritual perspective. We are truly spirit beings who are (as scripture teaches) made in God's likeness and image.

Regarding our Children

Many of us who work on the railroad have children at home that we don't get to see everyday. These thoughts came to mind one afternoon on March 14, 1994, while I was on the road:

What can be done to help our young people grow in the knowledge that all they need for an enjoyable, and full life is already within them?

How can we raise children to think critically, and not feel the need always to conform and be swayed by the crowd? How do we raise children so that they are content not only to be responsible, but just to BE?

We must trust, and show patience, and love. And we must live the principles that we want our young people to be guided by.

Thoughts Along The Way

"Why would a guy who writes and who has a college degree be working as an attendant on the train?" fellow passengers sometimes asked me. In all honesty, I don't know the answer, and it is not of great importance at this point in life. I recorded the following thoughts on June 6, 1993 while on-board *The Pioneer* traveling near Galesburg, Illinois:

Over much of my life I've assumed many roles. I've seen myself as father, son, spouse, teacher, student, brother, train attendant, and military officer, to mention a few. I've played a lot of roles.

But nowadays I identify less with roles and more with a sense of spirit within, which happens to be role-less. I have a growing awareness for the part of me that carries no title, the part that does not seek to make a statement or to prove anything to anybody. There's a feeling of contentment just knowing that I AM.

Race . . . a Slippery Concept

As we all know, race and ethnicity is a much discussed topic in America. It's written about in newspapers and magazines, talked about among friends, neighbors, and co-workers, and is often the source of controversy. I wrote the following words while traveling southbound on the Coast Starlight in September 1994:

There is no better way to keep a population divided than by perpetuating the notion of race. In these United States of America, few topics receive more press and more informal discussion than race and ethnicity.

We can direct attention to this topic until the end of time, but that does not make it a valid concept. For the most part, race is based on appearance, just as for many years it appeared that the earth was flat. Our behavior is frequently influenced by the appearance of race – that illusion, or pigment of the imagination which we so often act upon. Unfortunately, we're taught very early, as part of our social education, to give power to the appearance (or illusion) we call race.

Yet deep in our hearts we know that being black, white, or otherwise does not relate to anything that is real about someone. It says nothing about our character or our ability to experience joy and pain, nor does it speak to whether we extend ourselves to be of service to others. In our society, we're conditioned from an early age to see each other through distorted lenses that focus on the outer rather than the inner part of life. But when we let our hearts do the "seeing," we do not see race.

When I relate to others, I want my perceptions to be based on something real about them and not on some slippery idea of race.

Other Random Thoughts

Late one night, June 21, 1994, we were about to arrive at the Redwing, Minnesota, station. Though tired, I was joyful. It was day four of a six-day round-trip, and these are some words that came to mind:

I am best when I let myself BE, and focus on the spirit within. It's during these precious moments (like now) when I'm able to simply let God express through me.

It's very satisfying knowing that in order to feel the best, I need only to be aware of God's presence. I have a sense of freedom this moment that comes from realizing that to have real joy I don't need to take an ocean cruise, buy a new suit, eat, smoke a cigarette, or do anything at all. I need only to focus attention on the Christ spirit within and know that wherever I am, God is.

Redwing, Minnesota train station.

On the Railroad . . . in the Flow of Grace, April 1993

I usually like being on board, yet I feel anxiety whenever I leave home. It's a feeling that's intense, that words cannot fully describe.

But once I make the adjustment from being at home to being on the railroad, I achieve a certain peace. And I can sustain that peace as long as I resist the temptation to pass judgment upon others. The more I do what I have to do while not passing judgment about this or that, the better off I am. This seems to enable me to receive, and in turn to send out positive energy.

While I'm on the road, laughing, singing, playing my harmonica, and being of service all seem to come easy to me. Even in a difficult situation, it's easier to simply BE in the flow of grace once I've made the adjustment to being on the railroad.

Just Before Falling Asleep in the Employee Dormitory Car, February 25, 1995

When I relate to someone with my total energy focused in the present moment, I am aware that he or she is merely a creature of the universe, a child of God.

But when I allow my mind to get off track from the present moment, then and only then do I comprehend the language of race, gender, class, and other arbitrary categories that routinely divide us.

Feeling Stress

It was a few days before Christmas 1994, and I was sitting at home "unwinding" after an extraordinarily difficult trip. These words came to mind:

I'm convinced that it is especially important this time of the year to pray (as the apostle Paul says) "without ceasing." I'm sure that more than at any other time of the year, I would do well to make a point to live from within – that is, with an awareness of God's presence.

The material nature of our North American society is never more prevalent than during

This award-winning Amtrak Station serves Olympia-Lacey, Washington. It was built in 1993 with nearly all-volunteer labor, and is staffed daily with volunteer help,

*the Christmas Season. The emphasis is on
giving and receiving material things. The
frenzy of this preoccupation is stressful, to say
the least.*

*In some respects, this time of year brings sad-
ness to my heart. It makes me think of Christmas when I was a boy, when there were
Mother Dear, Daddy, David, Bobbie, Kathryn,
Vonnelle, June, and Sandra. Daddy and
Bobbie have made their transition from this
life, and at this time of the year I especially
think of them and miss hearing their voices.*

*At this very moment, though my body feels
great stress, I am lucky and blessed to be
aware that God is present here and now.*

Memorable Words of a Fellow Traveler

Sometime in early 1991, an elderly man on board shared his philosophy of life with me, as we conversed at brief intervals during the course of a trip on *The Pioneer*. When he left the train in Denver, he gave me a handwritten note with the following words:

The mind is influenced by our ego, and it in turn inflates the importance of our ego.

We must find a way to keep the mind focused on Truth, and not let the deceit of ego rule it.

The essence of us is spirit. Let us cultivate an acceptance of life (both in pain and pleasure).

It is for us to accept the gift of seeing, while being neutral and unremoved, or otherwise the mind will try to interpret the meaning of our experiences.

Mother Dear's Passing

From the time I was a small boy, my father trained my brother and me to address our mother as Mother Dear.

In late April 1995, Mother Dear died. And about three weeks after her passing, I was traveling northbound through Oregon's Willamette Valley on AMTRAK's *Coast Starlight*. I was tired and weary, and still feeling the pain of my mother's death. For a few moments that afternoon on May 14, 1995, I got

Gaynelle Mahon Porter
1915-1995

in touch with a feeling deep inside, and wrote the following words in my trip notes:

If there was ever a time when I felt that part of me had died, it was the morning I learned that my mother had just made her transition from this life. What an indescribable feeling of loss! And for a brief moment, what a deep feeling of insecurity just thinking of living in this world without the physical presence of my Mother Dear! Even writing about it in this moment makes my heart weep.

I know that Mother Dear's spirit will never leave me. By her own example, she gave SO MUCH, because she taught me to live by grace. It was she who taught me to be forgiving, understanding, and patient.

I'll do my best to walk with her in spirit, and carry a smile. But right now, as the thought hits me that I am unable to hear her soft voice or to watch her play the piano, there is a profound feeling of loss.

She now rests peacefully. I love her dearly.

Salt Lake City Train Station.

CHAPTER FOUR

The "How To" of Traveling by Train

Questions & Answers

What are some sources of information for traveling by train?

• Call AMTRAK reservations at 1-800-USA-RAIL. Check out their website on the Internet at:

  http://www.amtrak.com

• And if you don't have a home computer, it's worth stopping in at your local library and accessing the Internet. Anyone who is not familiar with travel by train will surely discover lots of useful information on the AMTRAK website.

• Check with a travel agent, and make sure it's one who is familiar with train travel. Many travel agents have never seen the in-

Newton, Kansas Union Station

side of a train, so be sure that the agent you select can offer firsthand information, aside from merely being able to sell you a ticket.

• http://www.trainweb.com
This Internet website offers probably the most complete one-stop source of AMTRAK train information available. If you want fares, schedules, accommodations, AMTRAK news, etc., you will find it here. If you're a model railroader, a rail fan, or simply an advocate for rail travel, this is also a good website to check out, with a wide selection of train-related books to order. This website is updated often, and will keep train enthusiasts current on a range of subjects.

Should I bring anything in particular on a long trip?

• If you're traveling in a coach car, it's a good idea to bring a blanket, as it can sometimes get a bit chilly late at night. Incidentally, the use of a neck pillow during long trips can also add to your comfort.

• Consider bringing fresh fruit and bottled water, as most food on board is prepared food, and drinking water is tap water drawn from the various AMTRAK watering locations along the route. If you want other than tap water, you can buy bottled water on-board or bring your own. Crew members almost always drink bottled water.

Why don't more people travel by train?

• Following World War II there was a deliberate effort in many areas of the country to make travel by train less convenient. By 1970, passenger rail travel had been all but eliminated – thanks to railroad companies that found it more profitable to transport freight rather than people, and to an automobile industry that capitalized on the nation's love affair with the private car. Finally, in 1971 Congress created AMTRAK, a semi-private corporation, and train travel once again became an option. No national passenger system in any country on the planet operates without substantial government support, yet our federal government (influ-

How Can You Help America Get Back On Track?

National Association of Railroad Passengers

(202) 408-8362

enced by powerful lobbies) doles out funds
only sparingly to AMTRAK. The result is that
the USA has a national rail passenger system in name only.

So consider joining a railroad passengers
advocacy group; or at least you may want
to write your congressmen and urge their
strong support for passenger rail travel.

How fast does the train go?

• The maximum speed of most AMTRAK
trains is seventy-nine miles per hour. However, the Metroliner between New York City
and Washington, D.C., and the Southwest
Chief between Chicago and Los Angeles both
exceed the 79 mile per hour speed at various
stretches along their routes.

Are there accommodations for handicapped and mobility-impaired travelers?

• AMTRAK has made a strong effort to accommodate persons who are elderly, or who
are in some way impaired. That's why there
is a downstairs section (with bathrooms) on
Superliner cars, so one does not have to climb

stairs. Also, most coach and sleeping cars have special equipment for handling wheelchairs. If you're going to need assistance, be sure to make it known to the clerk when you're booking reservations. And if there is a problem when you once board the train, ask to see the Chief of On Board Services.

To learn more about AMTRAK's provisions for the elderly and the disabled, write to: Office of AMTRAK Access, 60 Massachusetts Avenue, NE, Washington, D.C. 20002. You can request from that office a free copy of the booklet titled "A Guide to Amtrak Services for Travelers with Disabilities".

May I check my luggage to any scheduled station stop?

Almost all of Amtrak's scheduled station stops are manned, and therefore they can accommodate your checked baggage. BE-WARE, however, that there are occasional station stops on some routes that do not have Amtrak staffing. There are probably no more than about fifteen such unstaffed stations in the entire Amtrak system, and you should NOT check your baggage to one of these unstaffed stops (which are usually in very small towns). So if your destination is a very small town, then before checking your baggage, ask if your destination station is a staffed station that can accommodate checked baggage. If it is not staffed, then you will want to carry your baggage on-board with you.

"WORKS FOR ME."

When do train attendants sleep?

• On long haul trains, their work schedule is from about 5:30 A.M. until shortly after midnight, depending on the particular train. Train attendants for coach cars have berths in the employee dormitory car, and attendants for sleeping cars each sleep in the car to which they are assigned. If the train is delayed to any great extent, the attendants' sleeping schedule may vary. The bottom line is that TAs are to be on duty at the main scheduled stops. Needless to say, such a schedule can really take its toll on crew members, especially during the last two or three days of a long trip.

I'm scheduled to get off the train at around 3 A.M. If I'm asleep, will someone wake me up?

• Yes, you will be awakened by either the conductor, assistant conductor, or the train attendant. One of them will see that you get off at your stop, provided you are seated under your designated seat check containing the three-letter city code. If you're in the sleeper, a crew member will knock on your door in time for you to de-train at your station stop.

Where can I buy food on the train?

• The dining car sells three sit-down meals each day. The food is very tasty, and is well prepared. For breakfast, expect to spend from $5 to $7, for lunch from $6 to $8, and for dinner from $10 to $13. For light fare, sandwiches and snacks are available in the lounge car. If you desire fresh fruit, you'll need to bring that along, as most food on-board is cooked or processed.

What about the kids? Will they find the train a fun experience?

• In all likelihood, they will. Families are generally seated together, so children interact with other family members. Also, young

travelers are likely to meet other young people and strike up a friendship. Travelers young and old often spend time in the Lounge Car where a free movie is often shown once or twice during the course of a long haul trip.

The Coast Starlight, described by some rail fans as AMTRAK's premier western train, features a play room for smaller children. It offers toys and books, and occasionally, kids are treated to the special appearance of a real live magician.

May I take a stroll through the sleeper?

• Yes and no. Yes, if that's the car you are assigned to; and yes, if you are in another car and must walk through the sleeper to get to some other part of the train. But you may not walk through the sleeper just to "check it out." Remember, the sleeper car is a bit like a hotel on wheels, and passengers pay handsomely to be able to enjoy their privacy. If you have a strong desire to have a look at sleeping car accommodations, ask the attendant for that car to please show you one or two of the rooms when he or she is not busy.

What about accommodations for lap top computers phones?

• As of this writing, most of Amtrak's long distance trains do not have phones on-board. The one exception, however, is the *Coast Starlight* on the west coast. As for commuter trains, many of them currently have pay telephones on-board. Regarding laptop computers, the newest commuter trains have electrical outlets at each seat to accommodate laptops. However, Amtrak's Superliner and other older equipment have only a few outlets in each coach, so you'll need to contact your train attendant or the conductor. But all sleeper car accommodations (whether Superliner or older equipment) have electrical outlets to support laptops.

Where can I get off the train to make a phone call or simply to stretch?

• Ask a crew member for the location of the next service stop, where trains remain for fifteen to twenty minutes to take on water and fuel. You can make a phone call at that time, but remember to keep your conversation brief. Making phone calls at stops other than service stops are not recommended, because the train does not remain in stations for very long. Whenever you get off the train, unless you know that it's going to be in the station for a while, be sure to stay close enough to hear the "all aboard" signal. A word of caution: THE TRAIN WILL LEAVE, whether you're on it or not!

What about Y2K, the bug that might affect travel plans?

• By the time this book is in print we will have heard a lot about the "Y2K computer bug". To be sure, transportation systems (AMTRAK included) are certain to be affected by this global and system-wide problem. Many older mainframe computers, and millions of the tiny embedded hard-wired microprocessors, will "think" that 00 in the two-digit year-date field means 1900 instead of 2000. Clearly, that's bound to create problems! The mainframe computer is important for dispatching trains, and for tracking their location at any given time. On the other hand, tiny embedded microprocessors are used extensively throughout the train. These tiny embedded microchips control power generation and distribution, railroad signal switching devices, fuel flow in the locomotive engines, and they even regulate the temperatures in the refrigeration equipment in the dining cars. In short, these tiny microprocessors are literally all over the place, and many of them are date sensitive, which means that if they are not Y2K-compliant (i.e., if they "think" that year 2000 is the year 1900) then there could be problems.

• The Gartner Group, an international consulting firm that's been on the cutting edge of Y2K research, recently found that at least fifty percent of all businesses worldwide will experience mission critical computer failures in the year 2000. Software engineers have determined that there is not enough time remaining before the New Year (January 1, 2000) both to fix all the affected computer programs, and to locate and change the millions of non-compliant embedded microprocessors. Bottom line is that NO ONE can know for sure just how this problem will play out until January 1, 2000 and beyond!

• On July 25, 1999, the Seattle Times ran an article titled "How to Prepare for Y2K". It states the following regarding travel: "Avoid traveling New Year's Eve or early on January 1. If some problem crops up, this is when it will happen." In the same Seattle Times article, it recommends that if you're traveling during the end of the year 1999 to travel light, and try not to check- in any bags; that way, it is easier to change your travel plans while en route should the need arise. I PLAN NOT TO BE TRAVELING ON EITHER THE TRAIN OR THE PLANE DURING THE FIRST DAYS OF THE YEAR 2000. I emphasize, however, that this is my personal assessment, and not necessarily the official view of AMTRAK.

We just boarded the train at 6:15 P.M.. Dinner is being served in the diner. May we go there and eat after the conductor takes our tickets?

• Since dinner is served by reservation only, you should ask your train attendant to check with the dining car steward to find out what time is best for you to come for dinner.

Whom do I contact about upgrading from coach to sleeper car accommodations?

• Contact either the conductor or the assistant conductor. Be advised, however, that it may not be easy to upgrade, because sleeping car rooms are typically booked solid for months in advance. But if you're lucky enough to get a room on-board, you can often purchase it at a discount from the usual rate. The conductor can give you the details on this, depending on the particular train.

There are several empty seats in the next car. May I go sit in one of them?

• Passengers are loaded according to the conductor's loading plan. Check with the conductor or with your car attendant before changing seats, because they need to know where all passengers are seated in order to make sure that they get off at the right station stops. Also, remember that while the car next to you may not be full at any given time, there may well be plans for it to be filled with passengers a few stops away. So, again, check with a train crew member.

When train crew members are eating in the dining car, passengers sometimes walk by and say something like "YOU EAT, TOO?"

• If you get the urge to ask this question, think a minute. Crew members are human, too. So, please, don't ask.

What is the practice of tipping on board the train?

• When passengers eat in the dining car, they usually leave a tip, just as patrons in a regular restaurant do. Many sleeping car passengers also tip their attendant when they feel that satisfactory service has been rendered, and the amount they give is often $5 to $10 (sometimes more, sometimes less). Tipping in coach cars is less frequent, though on rare occasions passengers will tip their attendant for an especially good trip.

• Tipping is not required, and it remains an uncomfortable issue for some people. The really important thing is to try to be personable, and to show genuine appreciation for good service. How you do that is ultimately your choice.

What are some additional sources of passenger train information?

• Try the National Association of Railroad Passengers (NARP), 900 Second Street NE, Suite 308, Washington, DC 20002. It publishes a monthly newsletter dealing with rail travel issues of interest to the train traveler. Also try the National Railway Historical Society (NRHS) at P.O. Box 58153, Philadelphia, Pennsylvania 19102-8153. NRHS has chapters in major cities across the country, and they offer a wealth of information on train travel. And last but not least, Jack Swanson from Ouray, Colorado, has written Rail Ventures, a book packed with lots of interesting information for the AMTRAK train traveler.

A few AMTRAK facts taken from a 1994 news release

• AMTRAK trains travel over 25,000 miles of tracks daily. Most of these tracks are leased from various railroad companies.

• AMTRAK covered 48 percent of its operating costs in 1982; it covered 80 percent of its operating costs by 1993. AMTRAK, a private corporation whose stock is owned exclusively by the federal government, continues to earn a greater percentage of its operating costs.

• The federal government spends more than $6 billion a year on airports and aviation; it spends more than $23 billion annually on highways. In contrast, our government grudgingly spends roughly one-half a billion dollars per year on AMTRAK. It's important to note again that NO country in the world has a national rail passenger system that does not receive significant financial support from the government.

Is AMTRAK part of the Federal Government?

AMTRAK is technically a private corporation formed under the laws of Washington, D.C. It was created in 1970 by an act of Congress as the National Railroad Passenger Corporation. AMTRAK is not a federal agency nor is it an instrumentality of the federal government. However, since it receives considerable federal funding, it is therefore subject to federal oversight. The status of Amtrak and the official governing guidelines are set forth in Title 49, United States Code, Chapter 243.

What I'll Always Remember and Like About the Train

• Eating delicious food in the diner – patrons dine while observing a moving picture window. And I'll never forget the good smell of hotcakes as I entered the diner in the morning. Occasionally, as a crew member, I especially enjoyed eating downstairs in the kitchen where the cooks sometimes do their work to the soulful sounds of the likes of Otis Redding and Sam Cooke.

• The relaxed atmosphere – people are generally in a good mood, and many of them have a variety of interesting stories to tell.

• A view of the many faces of North America – mountains, the Great Plains, high-rise tenement houses in the cities, and yes – the back sides of buildings that are not so picturesque;

the views of people rafting on the Colorado River; scenes of people waving as the train goes by; the sight of a herd of deer in eastern Wyoming; or of a lone coyote in a snow-covered field in Minnesota.

• The Sightseer Lounge on the Superliner – it offers wide windows and a relaxing atmosphere where people congregate to enjoy conversation and laughter.

• And there's the magical feeling of retiring for the night in a sleeping berth where you're rocked to sleep to the rhythm of the train. I'll never forget that incredibly soothing motion!

A Closing Note

In times like these when we are increasingly alienated from one another because of differences in age, social class, ethnic background, profession, and geography, the train helps in a small way to rekindle a vital sense of community. It's true that the private automobile and electronics in general have enabled our society to make great technological leaps. But, unfortunately, the way we have used technology has resulted in the progressive loss of our sense of community. Thanks to the growing rediscovery of the train as a mode of travel, people in all walks of life now have a new opportunity to relate meaningfully to each other. Therein lies the Heart and Soul of the Train.

For your travel comfort, order a Bucky® U-Travel neck pillow

For those who like the cozy support around the neck and shoulders, there is this well-known neck pillow made by Bucky. It's light and compact for easy carrying (only 14 ounces) , and with stylish satin accent piping. This incredibly comfortable pillow, a favorite of the frequent flyer, is filled with light, movable, and soothing buckwheat hulls that conform to the perfect shape to cradle your head for relaxed snoozing on the train and elsewhere. It has a beautiful soft fleece cover that zips off for easy washing.

To order, copy this form and mail it to:

Apollo Publishing International
c/o P.O. Box 1937
Port Orchard, Washington [98366]

Date: _____

☐ Send me ____ copies of the book *Heart & Soul of the Train*, copyright 1999, at $9.95 per copy, and $3 for postage and handling. Reference, ISBN 0-9640125-5-3.
(No additional postage and handling when ordering more than one book).

☐ Send me ____ copies of the book *AMTRAKing*, copyright 1994, at $8.95 per copy, and $3 for postage and handling. Reference, ISBN 0-9640125-0-2.
(No additional postage and handling when ordering more than one book).

☐ Send ____ **Bucky** brand **U-Travel neck pillow** at $21.95 each, and $3 postage and handling
(No additional postage and handling when ordering more than one neck pillow).

Your Name _____

Address _____

City/State _____

☐ Enclosed is a check or money order in the amount of

$ _____ made out to: Apollo Publishing.

For further inquiries, e-mail us at: emekam@silverlink.net